A JOURNEY WITHOUT A MAP

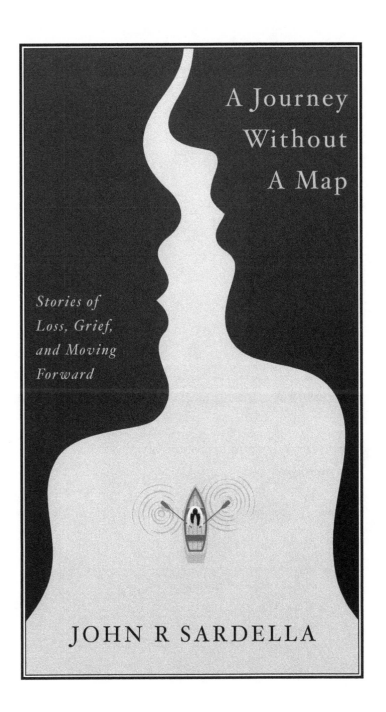

A Journey
Without
A Map

*Stories of
Loss, Grief,
and Moving
Forward*

JOHN R SARDELLA

LIONCREST
PUBLISHING

A JOURNEY WITHOUT A MAP
Stories of Loss, Grief, and Moving Forward

ISBN   978-1-5445-0754-5 *Hardcover*

978-1-5445-0753-8 *Paperback*

978-1-5445-0752-1 *Ebook*

978-1-5445-0755-2 *Audiobook*

This book is dedicated to my loving family, Megan, Harry, and Julia. And to the special person I lost—my wife, Margaret.

CONTENTS

INTRODUCTION

In April 2010, Margaret, my wife, had pain in her abdominal area. She went to the doctor to get it checked out, and they did an x-ray. They told her they'd call her if she needed to come back to the office for a follow-up. The next day, they called her at work and told her to come in. Margaret called me with the news, and I asked if she wanted me to come with her. She said she wasn't sure.

I got on the phone with the doctor's office myself to see if I should accompany Margaret. They said yes, they would recommend it.

I didn't know what that meant, but I would soon find out. We both would.

The next day, Margaret and I sat in the doctor's office.

We were anxious, but confident everything would be fine. The PA explained that they'd found a node in Margaret's abdominal area that needed more testing, and the staff took her out of the room for another x-ray. I asked the PA if it was serious, and she stated that it was. I knew no matter what, I needed to be there for Margaret every step of the way.

After that doctor's appointment, we went home and had as normal a day as possible. The real emotions started rolling in over the next couple of weeks. The doctor's office set Margaret up with an appointment with an endocrinologist to do an endoscopy and see what the node was. Our good friend Maureen accompanied us to the appointment. Margaret went under anesthesia and was examined. When she came out, she went to the recovery area and waited for the doctor.

When the doctor came in, he looked very serious. He stated the node was cancer of the pancreas, and they'd know more about its severity over the next couple of days.

After he left, Margaret turned to me with tears in her eyes.

"I don't want to die," she said.

I gave her a hug and told her she would be OK, that we'd

know more soon. I kissed her, and she closed her eyes to sleep a little more.

As she rested, I walked over to the window in the office, looked out, and cried.

Later, in the car, we cried together as we held each other and again said it was going to be okay. That was April 13, 2010.

The next day, the doctor called and sounded in good spirits. He told us the cancer had been tested and was a neuroendocrine tumor, one that was slow-growing and could be controlled. We were all hopeful in that moment.

We didn't realize then that our journey was just beginning. Our journey without a map.

* * *

Everybody has a defining moment in their life. For me, it wasn't when I lost my wife—which I did, on January 8, 2017, after a long battle with this ugly disease. My defining moment was when I *met* her, which started the incredible journey we took together.

That journey I mentioned—and what I've learned along the way—is what I will share with you in this book. Specifically, in the following pages, I will authentically share the story of my own grief after losing Margaret. Many of these moments were hard to recount in writing this book, but they need to be here because they're important. They're truths.

After Margaret died, I needed help coping. I looked for a book that would help me move through my grief in a way that both acknowledged the heartbreak and, ultimately, helped me *go forward*. I had difficulty finding a resource that did both, so I wrote one—for you, and for everyone else who is struggling to come to terms with a loss or is facing a challenge that feels heavy. This is that book.

Here, I will not only share stories of loss, but I will also share what (and who) helped me move forward. **That distinction is important because this is not a book of pity; it *is* a book of inspiration. This is not a book that says my way is the "only" way to process loss and work through grief; it *is* a book that says what worked for me.**

At the end of the day, I am a father, an educator, a member of my community, an author, a lacrosse coach, and Margaret's husband. I am offering you my stories of the past ten years—stories about the power of connection, faith, family, friends, and more—to help you navigate your own path, whatever that may look like. These are some of the important experiences of my life that have shaped me into the person I am today and that I know will help guide me on my journey in the future. I invite you to take from them what you need.

Chapter One

IT'S GOING TO BE OKAY

"I feel like I'm fading away. I'm ready to go. But I'm not ready for the sadness left behind. It's time to write my funeral."

—FROM MARGARET'S JOURNAL

The congregation appears before me as I stand at the podium, hundreds strong. The church is packed wall-to-wall, a sea of yellow.

We're here to celebrate the life of Margaret—the love of my life.

I'm holding a sheet of paper that holds my eulogy, the only speech I've ever written down. I look down at the piece of paper briefly, and I begin.

I can feel the strength from my children behind me and from the crowd of friends and family in front of me. I can also feel their collective sadness. It's deep. I feel the weight of it all. The last thirty years, of everything that's happened. Of the emptiness of loss, of those early days of confusion, and a feeling of numbness.

I take a deep breath, step to the microphone, and begin to eulogize my Margaret.

* * *

The kids and I pulled up to the church—fifteen minutes before the start of mass, just as Father O'Brien suggested—and saw cars everywhere. We ended up sequestered in a room with close family until we got the nod that the procession was to begin. Everyone was quiet and somber as we stepped in. We walked forward, all eyes on us, to the front rows of the church.

I heard the muffled sniffles of countless friends and family members. There was a traditional mass, and Margaret's siblings did the readings. After that, members of the congregation were called up to speak.

Gail, Margaret's sister, spoke. When I asked her to reflect on the experience as I was writing this book, she recalled, "I decided to write the eulogy as a letter because that was a big part of our relationship and who she was. She was always writing me letters and notes, so it felt appropriate to make the eulogy a letter to her. I'm still finding letters now, and I love it. I feel like it is so ironic that the letters she wrote me in 1982...said, 'I am always thinking of you, so don't be lonely. I miss you lots, and I love you.' That was the opening to my eulogy, and those words are incredible. Simple but true. I'm trying now to hear those words and try not to be lonely without her. The funeral summed up Margie [Margaret's nickname]. We were surrounded by what was important to her: her family, her friends, her church, and her prayer."

Margaret's childhood friend, Marialice, also spoke. She recalls of that moment, "I've never been asked to say some words at a funeral before. I was nervous. First, I'm not the best writer. Secondly, what could I possibly say that would do Margaret justice? How could I convey all that Margaret meant to me over the years, all that Margaret meant to her kids, her husband, her sisters? Mostly, I just wanted my speech to come from my heart, which was breaking at that moment. Margaret was my friend for as long as I could remember. We could talk about everything and anything, from books to boys and goals for our kids— *almost* anything. Margaret rarely talked about her illness. Instead, she wanted to talk about anything else. To this day, I cannot believe how positive she stayed through all the seven years. She had such grace and positivity. I was truly in awe of her. She made everyone around her feel special, especially me. Margaret had a way of letting you know she was listening to you. At the funeral and wake, I came to realize that I was not alone in feeling this way. That, in fact, Margie had made many people feel special. That was one of her gifts, one of many."

When it was our turn, I walked up with my three kids because we weren't sure who would be able to speak.

We saw the sea of people, the yellow, the sadness. I could feel people's hearts going out to us in love and support.

Then, our daughter Julia spoke. Julia is my youngest child. She stood at the podium with me and my other two children, Harry, who is the middle child, and Megan, the oldest. I stood behind her and rubbed her back as she read this eulogy.

> Jesus said to her, "I am the resurrection and the light. The one who believes in me will live. Even though they die, and whoever lives by believing in me will never die" (John 2). This week, Heaven gained the most kindhearted, passionate, compassionate, strong, and dignified angel that will ever appear at their gate. At the youthful age of fifty-one years old, my mom was able to have an impactful influence on countless individuals as a daughter, sister, wife, mother, teacher, and person.

My mom's everyday values and actions spoke volumes to the wonderful woman she will be remembered as. In the obscene quicksand of life, my mom maintained the hope that upheld herself and everyone around her. The closure of her journey is one to celebrate as her life was indescribably remarkable and special. My dad, brother, sister, and I will all have the most beautiful soul watching over us. The beauty of this angel is the precious hand that held my father's hand in marriage and each one of us at birth.

Her soul will continue to be with us through every walk of life, and when we're all ready, one day we will be together again. It is quoted anonymously, "Perhaps they are not stars but rather openings in Heaven where the love of our lost ones shine down to let us know they are happy." I miss you, Mom, and I love you without end.

Julia and her brother and sister stepped behind me. Megan placed her hand on my shoulder. It was my turn.

* * *

I stood there—my kids behind me—and opened with a joke. At the wake, many of the family pictures showed me having hair. (I used to have hair, but I turned forty, became a principal, and lost most of it.) Hundreds of people reminded me of that fact as they walked through the receiving line, busting my chops. So, that's what I led with at the funeral.

"I just want to thank everyone for letting me know that I used to have hair," I began.

Everybody laughed a little, which broke the ice and helped people to breathe a sigh of relief after having listened to the intensity of the eulogies. My goal was to make people laugh before they cried, and I was successful.

Then, I thanked everyone for their love and support, specifically family and some friends (Maureen, Kelly, Robin, and Kathy). I also thanked Mike LaCombe—or "La," as I call him—who had been my good friend since middle school and was also a radiation oncologist who had helped guide us through our seven-year journey. He taught us not to be a victim of the disease, but to control it and stay positive. He was also the one who told us what we were facing: a journey without a map.

I continued by telling those in attendance that it's okay to be sad, to cry, and to have all the feelings they were experiencing. I said I had only one ask: that they not be angry, because anger wouldn't solve anything.

"And it's going to be okay," I said then. I knew I had to give the permission to grieve, including to myself. I then thanked Father O'Brien for his relationship with Margaret and the strength they had together in going through this journey with the power of God and the church.

I ended by saying, "As we go through this journey, we'll continue to support each other—we will support you as you support us, and we'll get through it together. May God bless each and every one of you."

My children handled the wake and service with grace and dignity, and I couldn't be prouder of them. They helped people smile. Throughout the entire service, no one mentioned the word 'cancer.' That's what Margaret wanted.

MARGARET'S FUNERAL PLANS

Before she died, Margaret took time to write down her wishes for her funeral. Her directions weren't extensive: she wanted to have a mass. She wanted to include the song "Spirit in the Sky," which played during the recessional. She wanted her sister Patty and her brother Tommy to do the readings. She did not want her illness mentioned, because she didn't want her struggle to be the focus. Instead of the traditional dreary black of funerals, Margaret wanted people to wear yellow, which speaks to her endless optimism and love of life.

She also wanted me to be the only one to speak, but I felt compelled to let others speak as well—the only instance in which I didn't follow her exact wishes. I knew there were other special people in her life who could share in that moment, and it felt appropriate to give them the space to do that.

THE FINALITY OF DEATH

I remember the moment Margaret died. As she lay there slowly breathing, I told her it was okay to go, and we would be okay. Before she went into an unconscious state, I said, "I love you," and she said, "Love you." Then, she went to sleep.

When she stopped breathing, the kids and I—the only ones in the room at the time—just wept. The grief was deeper than any feeling I'd ever experienced before—so deep that sometimes, my tears felt like they came all the way from my toes. I remember my mind racing, thinking to myself, *How am I going to get through this, and how are the kids going to get through this?*

Her death offered a finality to what she'd gone through for the last seven years. I knew immediately that she'd gone to Heaven and didn't have to deal with the pain and suffering any longer.

After Margaret took her last breath, we had to wait for the doctors to come in and confirm her death. Everyone left one at a time, and I was the last one there. I kissed her on the forehead and went home. In a way, I knew what to expect because of the experience of my father's death in 2002. When he died, a big part of my mother died with him. For the following sixteen years, until her death, she didn't change anything about the house where I grew up. His cowboy hat was still on the dresser. She still had clothes in his closet. I was always respectful of when she wanted to clean it all out, saying, "Mom, when you're ready, we'll do this."

She was never ready.

In my case, after Margaret died, I went home and had to face the empty house full of memories. The people who were in town—the brothers, sisters, and friends at the house—all scattered and went home to prepare for a return trip for the wake and funeral.

I stood in our bedroom, holding kitchen garbage bags. I stared at the pill bottles on the nightstand, the cancer drugs. I went there first, literally filling up two kitchen garbage bags full of the medicines from her nightstand alone. That's how many she'd taken. I broke down in that moment, crying so hard I couldn't catch my breath.

I knew I had to change the room. The next day, I asked Megan, Julia, and Gail to go through all of her belongings and keep whatever they wanted. We gathered the other clothing to take to the rescue mission. I cleaned out the bedroom because I knew if I kept it the same way, I would never be able to move on—a lesson I'd learned from my mother. I'll share more of this story in chapter five when we talk more deeply about moving on.

THE GRIEVING PROCESS

Even though she was going through so much pain and so much anguish through this journey, Margaret's physical presence offered some comfort when she was still alive. I could hold, hug, and love her. I could talk to her. When she was gone, it was much sadder. Even though I watched her demise from 2010 to 2017, there was still some joy. Even in the last six months, we had a party for Julia when she graduated from high school, and Margaret looked fantastic in those pictures.

A couple weeks later, she had an interventional treatment that involved putting micro balls into her liver. Then, I watched her lose twenty pounds and get so weak that she went out on her own and got a walker. She knew she wouldn't be able to walk on her own, and I had to help her upstairs. I stood behind her as she walked upstairs so she didn't fall backward. I tucked her in every night. Still, I didn't feel the same emotion when she was going through it as once she was gone, because she was still physically there.

Her disease was always at the forefront of my thinking.

I'd go to work and think about her and what she was going through. I'd tap my forehead and say, "It's always right here." When she was gone, that grief spread all around my brain. It permeated. It's a part of everything now, and I know I'm not the only one who feels that way. I also know I'm not the only one for whom "it's going to be okay" resonated so deeply.

Six months after Margaret's death, I received a note from Beth—a teacher who worked under me my first year as principal. She became a principal in another district as well as a good friend, and she had attended Margaret's funeral. She wrote, "I could have listened to Margaret's sisters and best friend for hours. They captured her essence and spirit in a way that I had never seen before. I can see why when you addressed the congregation that you said it's going to be okay. When nothing but love remains, I guess that is so."

Those words rung true for others, too. Marialice reflected, "I remember the beautiful words Julia said about her mom and the words John said at the end, that the family would get through this, that they would be okay, to remember the good times and not to wallow in the hardships. That's what Margaret would have wanted."

Even though it's been almost ten years as of this writing—seven years of her illness and three without her—my grief is still there. It will always be. But it does change over time, which is one of the reasons I'm writing this book. To show you, like I told Margaret and like I said in my eulogy, that it's going to be okay.

Chapter Two

THE POWER
OF YELLOW

"John just smiled and said, 'It will continue all day. You're special, and people are showing support.' While it's hard and it makes me emotional, why can't I just be happy about it, not teary-eyed? Well, I choose to be thankful. I too am wearing my yellow sweater and my beloved Chuck Taylors, now 28 years old, a gift from John R. Let the day treatment begin. Father O'Brien was all about marrying our blessings and gratitude. It was perfect."

—FROM MARGARET'S JOURNAL

Margaret loved the color yellow, as it represented her optimistic and sunny spirit. At her funeral, someone—I still haven't figured out who it was—handed out 100 yellow roses. But that wasn't all the yellow that was there. Almost everyone had gotten the memo: that we'd be celebrating Margaret, and we'd be doing it in yellow.

In fact, Ben, Margaret's godson, recalls of the wake, "Walking into her lifelong parish, there stood her family. Her daughters wore bright yellow dresses and her son and husband flashed yellow ties. As the night went on, countless people flooded through the doors. They all wore something yellow. So many people came to pay their respects, and the wake went on for hours beyond its schedule. This was no ordinary wake. However, this was the celebration of my godmother, Margaret Sardella...They chose to celebrate her life with optimism and not sorrow."

Optimism is something we carried with us throughout Margaret's journey with this ugly disease. We wanted to keep life as normal as possible, especially for the kids, and were intentional about how much we shared—which, in the beginning, wasn't much.

SHARING THE NEWS

For a long time, we kept Margaret's illness close to the vest. She didn't feel comfortable being seen as a person with cancer—not because there's anything wrong with that, but simply because she didn't want to be singled out. This decision and focus on privacy bothered many people, because they thought they had the right to know what was going on.

Margaret and I were both visible community members due to her work as a teacher and my work as a principal. People in our buildings had a general sense of what was going on. I might say I needed to take Friday off to go to the Dana-Farber Cancer Institute for her treatment, for instance. However, I kept my sharing simple, without going into a lot of detail.

Many coworkers felt fine about my approach, but others wanted to know more. Because I managed sixty-five people, there was the potential for anything I said to turn into gossip. I also knew some of the people in my building lived in my neighborhood, and telling one of them the details of our journey would mean everyone finding out, which we strongly wanted to avoid. Even though we knew our friends and coworkers would be supportive, we didn't want the attention or sympathy. We wanted each other. We wanted our life.

We also wanted to keep life as normal as possible for our children. Margaret felt adamant about not wanting people to look at her kids as "the kids whose mother has cancer." Our approach may not be shared by every family, but for us, the less we talked about her illness in public, the more power we had to control the narrative and experience for our kids. Some adults didn't understand our approach, though, and would ask the kids questions about their mom, which really bothered them. In these cases, we'd have to reassure the kids that we were working through the issue as a family and could keep the experience between us.

When Margaret was diagnosed, the kids were young. Megan was a junior in high school, Harry was a freshman, and Julia was in sixth grade. Though we wanted to keep life normal as possible for them, they knew it was different. A lot of Margaret's aversion to the visual signs of support and being the center of attention came from her desire to protect the kids. This is because when people hear you have cancer, they immediately want to donate money or make dinner for you. Their reaction was difficult for me initially, because it started almost immediately when she was diagnosed. At the time, if you saw Margaret, you wouldn't have known she had cancer. She looked perfectly healthy and fine. She still worked out, stayed active, and taught. She lived her normal, active life.

The first time someone brought us dinner, it bothered me. Margaret talked to me and helped me see that people just wanted to support us. I had to make peace with their actions because I knew they'd increase more as we went through her treatment. I thought, *We don't need this,* whereas my wife thought, *They're being so nice.* That's just another example of who she was.

We found that most people's reactions to the news, once they learned it, were temporary. They wanted to do fundraisers, but we didn't need a fundraiser. We both had good salaries and health insurance. We paid very little for her care, and when you enter a clinical trial—which we did—you don't pay for anything. Our true friends stayed through the whole process rather than acting in a flurry of wanting to help and then disappearing. They represent the meaningful, important relationships to hang on to and discuss more in chapter four. I like to say it's not about the quantity of friends you have; it's about the quality of friends. It's about having the right people around you. At this time in our lives, we noted everyone's well-intentioned offers to help, but we made sure to keep the right people around us.

SUPPORTING MARGARET

As the cancer spread, Margaret was set to begin a new treatment—this time, it would be an IV chemo regimen, the first in IV form she'd had up to that point in her journey. I knew we had to lift some of the privacy and invite people to support her because her treatment was intensifying, and she also had to take five months off from teaching for the first time. There was no keeping that a secret. Having a teacher out of the classroom for that long is a big deal, and people wanted an outlet to support her.

Only then, for her first IV treatment, I felt it was time to call on family, friends, and our school communities to offer her additional support.

I sent out messages to her staff, my staff, and friends and family, asking them to send photos of them wearing the color yellow to Margaret's cell phone during the day of her treatment. She had no idea.

As we arrived at the infusion center and she settled in, Margaret started to receive the messages.

Her initial response was, "Oh, that's nice. People are sending me pictures."

But then, as they kept coming, she began to realize what was happening.

There were photos of individuals wearing yellow. Photos of families wearing yellow. Photos of my staff wearing yellow and holding up a sign that read, "Stand strong, Margaret. We will stand with you."

All in all, Margaret received about 100 photos that day,

all from those who cared about her and wanted to show it. The support was phenomenal and so uplifting.

BEING A SUPPORT PARTNER

I told Margaret from day one that she would never be alone in this fight. I told her I'd be there every step of the way, and I was. I went to almost every doctor's appointment and every CT scan.

The first three years, Margaret's cancer was controlled. The doctor's visits were fairly routine. Right before Christmas in 2013, though, everything changed. The cancer had metastasized, and the doctor told us we'd be shifting our focus from the pancreas to the liver. From that point on, Margaret shifted from a fairly standard routine of oral chemo and stabilizers to what would total nine different treatments until her death in January 2017.

The changing diagnosis brought with it a change in the intensity of her medications. We went back to Dana-Farber for another clinical trial, which worked at first but then stopped working. She could feel none of the treatments were making a difference, but she still went for regular weekly or biweekly visits, locally or in Boston. Ninety percent of the time, I went with her; the other times, a close friend or her sister did.

The news that the cancer had spread completely shocked us. We'd gotten used to three and a half years of hearing positive news. The cancer had stabilized and seemed to be shrinking. The doctor had even spaced her CT scans out to four months because she seemed to be doing so well. Hearing this news two days before Christmas felt especially devastating. We were very emotional. It was difficult to get through the holiday, but we put on a brave face and made sure the kids were okay.

We didn't want to feel pessimistic, but it was hard not to. My father died of liver cancer, and the doctors back then were amazed he lived an additional three years. When Margaret's cancer spread, I knew she'd die in the next few years. From then on, the visits felt somber, characterized by nervous anxiety, sadness, and the unknown. One good visit wasn't good enough to cheer us.

For just over three years, we were on a roller coaster: the CT scan after one round of a treatment would generally show positive results, such as a shrinkage or stabilization. Then, the next CT scan would *sometimes* show more marginally more positive results, but usually not. If not, we'd be onto another medication.

Margaret's oncologist, Dr. Wong, was incredible, and he did everything he could. Because nothing was helping, though, it was like he was throwing darts in the air. We were trying to find something to stick, something to work.

The office visits became a guessing game, and they were often brutally painful for Margaret and I. When the doctor came in, we could sense from his tone and demeanor how the CT scan results had come back. He'd be excited for positive results and heartbroken for negative ones, sometimes even crying with us there in the room.

As the visits changed, my role as a support person changed, too. I'd always been there for Margaret, but it was more than that after these painful visits. We'd go to the car, and she'd cry, saying, "What's next?" I'd hold her in those moments, not leaving her side. She knew she was getting closer to the end after each doctor visit, and it was incredibly painful for me to watch that realization in someone I loved so dearly. She was everything to me.

In 2015, Margaret was in a lot of pain and went to the hospital. I asked the doctor if I should be contacting hospice. He said he thought she'd get out that time, but he made sure to tell me that whenever she did stop treatment, she'd die within three weeks. He wanted me to be prepared. Around this time, we started to have blunt conversations with the doctor. He'd tell us we needed to get our affairs in order and tell the kids, for example. The toll of this roller coaster ride was devastating. Sometimes we'd even have to go back to work afterward, having had such heartbreaking talks.

MY FATHER'S EXPERIENCE

Seeing my father's experience helped me better understand Margaret's.

My father battled cancer for many years; the last four years of his life, it metastasized to his liver. He continued to be active for as long as he could; he retired, he traveled everywhere from Las Vegas to Texas to Spain. He made sure he had quality experiences with my mom and kept his life relatively normal. He died in December 2002, when he was seventy-three.

Watching from afar, I was a little naïve. My mother was by his side the whole time. As he deteriorated in November of 2002, my siblings, my kids, and I all went to the house and had a Thanksgiving meal. My father was in bed, but he got up for dinner. I had a feeling he'd be gone soon. I put the Christmas lights up on the outside of the house, and my brother Rick showed up. I told him he needed to go inside and tell our dad how much he meant to him, and I believe he did. I could sense there wasn't much time left. I also sat by my father's bed and told him I loved him and how much he meant to me. The day after Thanksgiving, he ended up in the emergency room. Two weeks later, I watched him take his last breath.

I helped my mother every day, making sure I was there as he went through the final stages of life. This experience taught me a lot about the importance of being physically present—both for my father and mother. I didn't want either of them to feel alone.

When my father passed away, I was thirty-nine years old and had never watched someone die before. I was devastated because my father was immensely important to me. And—even though I drove him nuts—I had the closest relationship with my father of anyone in my family. When he died, each of my family members left the room, and I was there alone with him. I told him I loved him, kissed him goodbye, and walked out. Later, I eulogized him. Now, I've been there for the deaths of three people: both my parents and my wife. The experience elicits mixed feelings. I know they're all at peace and going to Heaven, and they're in a better place. At the same time, the feeling of loss is overwhelming.

I specifically recall leaving the hospital after my father died. I'd just left his room. Walking out those front doors, I felt like the world would stop. I'd walk past people on the sidewalk or see a car go by, and I had this overwhelming realization that people had no idea what I'd just experienced. I'd just left my father. My father who died. And these people were out here living like nothing happened.

This was a hard lesson: life goes on. It doesn't stop. The activity around us continues even when we feel stuck in our grief.

I knew what happened to my father would happen to Margaret, and I knew I had to support all the people around me and help them understand she'd be gone sooner than later. That realization helped me to say to my kids, family, and friends around me, "When she passes, you're going to walk out there, and life is going to continue. You have to keep moving on and progressing forward. No matter how difficult it is, life doesn't stop."

DON'T BE A VICTIM

Dr. Mike LaCombe, whom I call "La," was one of those close friends I thanked when I eulogized Margaret—and for good reason. He taught both of us *a lot*—namely, not to be a victim.

I met La when we played basketball together in middle school, and we've stayed close ever since. In adulthood, he became a radiation oncologist. This made him not only a good, lifelong friend, but also our guide throughout Margaret's cancer journey. He gave us advice about what to expect at visits, tips on what questions to ask, and perspective on navigating the journey—a journey which, as I mentioned at the beginning of this book—he was the *first* to call "one without a map." We'd send him the scans and other information from her doctor, and he'd double-check them. Often, he just affirmed what Dr. Wong had said; his emphatic agreement with and confidence in the plan helped immensely.

La told us that many people hear the word cancer and immediately become a victim of that disease. He encouraged Margaret to take the opposite approach. "You control it," he told her. "You have the ability to control your life and to move on." That advice meant so much to us that I even mentioned it in my eulogy. It guided us.

La was important to us because he not only was there for the cancer part, but he was there for the "life" part, too. Two months before we first traveled to Boston for treatment—when we didn't quite know what to expect—La invited us and the kids to vacation with his family at the Outer Banks. To this day, the kids and I will never forget that five-day stay. It allowed us to forget our troubles for a bit.

Throughout Margaret's journey, La served as an important resource for us; there were times I had very honest conversations with him about what he expected to happen next. He kept a positive outlook, but I also knew he'd tell us the truth, even if it was hard. What he said was gospel to us, and we lived off his input because we had 100 percent trust in him. So, when he said "don't be a victim," we took that advice to heart. We adopted that attitude and sustained it moving forward.

TAKEAWAYS

Surgery was never an option for Margaret, but for the first four years of her battle, we truly believed she'd live with treatments for many years to come—even well into our retirement. We didn't look at the reality of death until the last years of her life. Even then, we tried to keep that optimism going—especially for the kids.

I titled this chapter "The Power of Yellow" because it speaks to Margaret's endless optimism, in both good times and bad. She loved the color. She'd often buy yellow clothes. Yellow was the color of our family room at one time. She wanted a yellow front door, and I regret never painting it that color for her. I should have.

One Christmas, we bought a yellow VW Bug for her—a great present. It was both hilarious and impractical, since we had three kids and it only sat four people. It didn't last long, but it made her smile.

I'd often buy Margaret yellow roses, and she'd put them throughout the house. Sometimes, I still put yellow roses out because they remind me of her.

I feel I did everything in my power to help Margaret. I supported her first by letting people know she was fine and not making the illness a bigger deal than it already was. When I asked friends not to make public gestures like selling bracelets or having fundraisers, they may have thought I was the one saying no. But I was always doing it for Margaret.

If you're supporting someone with cancer or another serious illness, I advise focusing on being physically present. Sometimes you don't have to do anything other than stand by the person's side so they don't feel like they're struggling alone. Simply seeing the color yellow made Margaret happy. Find out what makes your loved one happy, and try to do as much of that as you can.

Also, try to keep life as normal as possible. I encourage you not to be a victim of the disease or your circumstance, even though I *know* it's hard sometimes. Trust me. Just fight it and keep moving forward. It is also worth it to ask what kind of support your friend or loved one wants. Maybe they want an outpouring of attention, or maybe they don't. Don't assume. In our case, public gestures too early would have worried our kids because we didn't even know the extent of what we were facing yet, so it would've been impossible to explain it. It's very important to respect the patient and ask permission. Then, when the time is right—in our case, for Margaret's first IV chemo treatment and the shower of yellow—it means even more, because it's wanted.

Chapter Three

THOSE LEFT BEHIND

"The doctor was quite somber today, I didn't like that! He asked me if I have had a conversation with the kids. I didn't like that."

—FROM MARGARET'S JOURNAL

Margaret and I found that when communicating with our kids and close friends and family, it was important to deliver information in an honest and age-appropriate way. That was hard when we didn't necessarily always have all of the information. We didn't know what would come next, but we did our best. I've found parenting children through grief and loss is an experience unlike any other.

CONVERSATIONS

The discussion prior to Margaret's death was heart-wrenching, to say the least. In December of 2016, we determined Margaret would not have any more treatments. She and I spoke about letting the kids know. Julia was home from college, as was Harry, but Megan wasn't coming home until December 23rd. We waited until then.

We asked the kids to come into the family room, and Margaret did most of the talking. She spoke about how things had changed and that she was closer to dying. She knew she was close to her end. Each of the kids broke down one at a time. There were heavy tears, heavy emotions. There was sadness along with confusion, anger, and disbelief. I then told the kids Christmas would be as normal as we could make it, as we had to enjoy the time we had.

We did have an as-normal-as-possible Christmas that year: taking pictures of the kids on the stairs, opening presents, and staying together all day. On January 1, 2017, Margaret went to the ER, and she never came home again. She died a week later, on January 8th.

Ultimately, Margaret passed away two weeks after Christmas. It was so important for us as a family to focus on having a last, good holiday together. We needed something positive to work toward in the face of the horrible news. This is a small example of the mentality that we have the ability to control what we think and do. Through this whole experience, we chose not to be victims.

TELLING THE KIDS

Obviously, the conversation before Margaret passed was a heartbreaker, but there were many other conversations we had with the kids leading up to that point and at various points in Margaret's battle.

At first, when Margaret was first diagnosed, we needed to determine the first steps in fighting the disease before we could tell anyone. When we decided to go to Dana-Farber in Boston, our first discussions with the kids related to our plans to travel to the cancer institute every other week to see the doctor. At first, we only talked to our older children in high school, Megan and Harry, because Julia was just getting ready to start seventh grade.

In writing this book, I talked with each of them about their impressions of those initial conversations and their mom's journey, as a whole. These talks blew me away. My kids were real with me about the impact the experience had on them.

We hadn't had the conversations earlier for a combination of reasons. First, I don't think they knew how to articulate their experience in the initial aftermath. They're also somewhat guarded around me because they don't want to upset me. In the past, I have tried to talk about Margaret and bring up different memories; usually, we'll chuckle a little bit, but then tuck those moments away and move on. Part of the journey includes not knowing what to say or do; we're all just trying to figure it out. By now, you know there is no map.

This book has given us the opportunity to talk about our experience and for them to truly share. These discussions—which I will share with you now in part—have been incredibly powerful for me in terms of giving me perspective and also helping our family heal.

MEGAN'S EXPERIENCE

Megan wasn't able to fully process what was going on with her mom. When Margaret and I had that first conversation with her and Harry, Megan says she never felt it was *that* serious. She knew her mom would be okay. Sometimes, though, she'd go for a run and feel lonely and scared about the uncertainty of it all. She recalls that when we traveled for treatment and left her in charge, that was hard for her. She also remembers my telling her that if she ever had a party when we were away, she'd be in big trouble—a recollection that made us both laugh.

Megan feels like the experience made her grow up immediately, helping to shape her into the mature, responsible adult she is. As a senior, Megan lived at home for the first year of Margaret's illness. Back then, though, she felt guarded and didn't let people in easily, sometimes feeling like she didn't have an outlet. Some of the small things that would bother her friends, Megan found petty. She wondered how they could get bogged down by minor issues. Margaret's cancer gave Megan perspective right away to understand the big picture instead of sweating the small stuff.

To this day, Megan doesn't take anything for granted. Going away to school (Wagner College on Staten Island) helped her become who she is. She made friends with people who had been through the same kind of adversity she was experiencing, and she felt less alone.

As Margaret was going through her last two years and declining, she changed physically. Megan would be away at school and come home every couple of months; seeing the drastic changes in her mother shocked her. She recalls these visits as highly emotional.

When her mom took a turn for the worse, Megan felt empty. Luckily, she recalls that she had the support of her boyfriend, and she always stayed in good communication with her mom and me. She says she was not surprised by the loss, but still felt shocked. "There's a hole that will never be filled, because all my worst fears came to pass," she said.

After Margaret died, Megan committed to coming home

once a month to be with me and help. Today, she looks at the future without her mom and sees it as unfair. She misses simply calling her mom and learning from her mother's experiences at her age, and she wishes they'd spent more time together. She misses her mom's smile and her hugs. Megan is currently engaged, and she says getting married without her mom scares her.

HARRY'S EXPERIENCE

Harry has always had a deep intuition about what's going on around him. The first time Margaret and I talked to him about her diagnosis, he knew *something* was up. He remembers feeling sad and confused, going upstairs to lie down next to Margaret after he heard the news. He felt helpless, not knowing the extent of the problem. Would it be one month and then cancer-free, or was it going to keep going?

On December 23, 2016—the day we told the kids Margaret was going to die—Harry recalls that it didn't quite register. Mentally, he didn't want to accept it and tried to block it out. He remembers me saying, "Let's make this a great Christmas." He obviously noticed that his mom looked less healthy, and that Christmas was tough. On January 1, 2017—his twenty-second birthday—we brought Margaret into the hospital for the final time.

Harry recalls that the hardest part, for him, was going

back to Coastal Carolina for college upon learning his mom didn't have much time left. He remembers they said they loved each other, he waved to her, and she had enough energy to wave back. He expected her to die during his semester, but he wasn't sure when. He left on January 7th. Eight hours after he left, I called him to come home and say goodbye to his mother.

On the morning of the 8th, Harry was struck by how much Margaret had changed. She'd gone from talking and saying goodbye to lying there, neither breathing well nor sleeping. He recalls looking at her and breaking down, the deepest emotion he's ever experienced. He didn't expect such a shocking change in such a short time.

When I asked him what he misses about his mother, he said, "Everything."

JULIA'S EXPERIENCE

Julia says she doesn't remember the first time Margaret and I spoke to her about the diagnosis—ironically, because we didn't. As the memories came back, she wasn't part of that conversation. Her junior year of high school, she remembers feeling upset and shocked upon learning we were heading to Dana-Farber, but she didn't realize the seriousness of the situation.

As she grew and headed to college, she remembers the changes in her mother appeared starker with every visit. Her first semester of college was Margaret's worst time, when she had the most intensive treatment—the chemo balls directly implanted in the liver. Margaret was a 5'6", 115-pound lady, and she lost twenty-five pounds—very visible on such a light person.

It was more than weight loss. Margaret's skin changed, and her hair thinned. Julia says she felt scared and sad. Julia says she only understood the severity of the situation when we all sat down on the couch on December 23, 2016, to tell the kids Margaret was dying. Children often think their parents will be there forever, and this was no different.

When Margaret went to the hospital shortly after that Christmas, Julia thought she'd come home like before. Then, she realized this time would have a different outcome. There was no chatting or playing cards in the room—only sleeping. Julia knew her mom was going to die.

Julia says she can't fully describe the feeling except as emptiness, like time stopped. Everything felt like it was moving along outside of her, but inside the room, time seemed to stand still. The experience she described sounds much like mine when I left my father's hospital room after he died.

Now, Julia—who was exceptionally close with her mother and who I used to call 'Mini Mommy' or 'Mini Margaret'—says the world feels strange. She's used to her mom not being around, but when she sees other families, it hits her.

DEEPER REFLECTIONS FROM JULIA

Recently, Julia sent me an email to further describe her experience. In part, it stated:

Dad, when you asked me about my feelings in those particular occasions of our past, I found myself speechless. I think this comes from the fact that we went through truly indescribable pain. Here is my best way to describe it. The first time, the actual first account I can remember regarding Mom's illness, was on the Soule Road Elementary playground [where Margaret taught, and the kids went to school].

I was in sixth grade, and Mom had been out of school for a few days as you both were discovering the results of her stomach pain. A former teacher of mine, and Mom's coworker, asked me about her. I said she was fine, as I was unaware of the seriousness of what was happening. This would be my response for years to follow. I find myself using the word "fine" often, and, most importantly, the meaning stands for nothing that is actually fine.

The second time that stands out to me is February of my junior year when Mom's symptoms got worse. At this time, they recommended the need to go back to Dana-Farber biweekly. Parallel to this time, I was in the final process of committing to college, and I was told we may not be able to make my visit anymore. I was taken over with a lot of emotions and decided I needed to talk to somebody about it. That's when I went to my best friend Cassidy.

When I sat down on her living room couch, I was crying and tried to begin to tell her about Mom's condition. As I began to utter the words, Cassidy stopped me, shaking her head up and down, telling me she was already aware of it.

This is how my conversations with people go for the next two years. It was something that a lot of people knew about, yet I had no idea they knew. Each time that someone was aware of it, I was hit with a wave of emotions: this was something bigger than I knew how to wrap my head around.

* * *

When you and Mom sat Harry, Megan, and me down on the couch that night in late December [2016], time actually felt like it froze. The moments after you delivered the news, I found myself sitting on the couch with Cortland [our dog], unable to comprehend what I had heard. I felt fear. I felt quite literally like the world was just thrown into my face. Our home just came crashing down upon all of us. Since that day, nothing has been normal.

The days of visiting the hospital went by, and it was constant worry. I would leave the hospital after a visit and say to myself repetitively, "I will see her tomorrow. I will see her tomorrow." The day came where I realized how severe it was when I walked into the hospital room and she was not responsive and unable to stay awake. I can genuinely say that this is the actual moment in time that I realized how serious the situation was, because it happened so fast.

On the morning of January 8th, it felt...like I was watching myself out of a movie. I found myself watching our car drive home, away from the hospital, in disbelief. It felt like a dream, like everything was just in my head. Yet, when time was frozen for us, life was bustling for everyone else that morning. We were then all faced with the demands of life because time did not freeze; this was now our reality.

In the few years since our loss, I find that grief and pain come in waves. Not a single hour of the day goes by without a thought of mom, but this is just the reality of my future. The thoughts will never stop, and the pain will never stop. However, some days are easier than others. For me, it is the little things that are the most significant in not only my memories, but reasons for missing her today. I mention that I am now the only female in the house. It has hit me slowly how much I miss having a female figure prominent in my life every day. The memories of our relationship I cherish every single day. I've grown to embrace the color yellow and let it inspire me to have happy days. Mom always told me I needed to smile more and embrace how lucky I am. I finally have a grasp on that. Reflecting on the way she carried herself through her 51½ years will always be my biggest inspiration and guide.

There are times of loneliness and sadness quite often, times that I wish I could have realized how serious it was earlier, and times that I regret how I acted as I was still growing and developing the maturity I maintain now. These times make me wish that I had more time with her. These times are teaching me the ways that I should act as I continue into my future. It is my current age now [twenty-one at the time of this writing] that daughters truly understand and appreciate the gift of their parents. I think that notion will always leave me with a feeling of heartbrokenness.

I also mention how it feels normal. By normal, I mean that we have adjusted to this life. When a tragedy strikes, time does not stop but really seems to start to move faster. We are fortunate to get back on our feet and find a way to walk through the rest of the walks of our life. For now, my physical life at home is with a single parent. I have learned to accept that and find normalcy with it. The outside world is unaware of the craziness of these past few years, but that's okay, they don't need to know because it's our craziness and I wish it upon no one.

My physical, seeable life is a whole lot different than one I lived within my own head. My mom is always with me, although not seeable. Not a moment goes by when I don't wish things were different, but strength has gotten me to accept the past and learn from it. I cherish the memories we have, and now live with the understanding of how precious every breath is. Pain, suffering, loss, and grief are all feelings that are merely indescribable and impossible to fully encompass in a string of words.

MY EXPERIENCE

I not only had to communicate at all these points to my children, but I also had to digest this information myself. My personal journey went from confusion, to wondering *why us*, to then understanding death. In October of 2016, I realized Margaret would die sooner than later. In some ways, this realization was emotionally freeing. I could comprehend that death happens in life. When mentally, you're always challenging yourself to think positively, look on the bright side, and be strong for everybody else, you get to a point where you live what you believe. I was able to do that, but I also gained perspective when I broke it down: life means being born and then dying. Everyone's journey in between is different. Margaret died at fifty-one. It could've been at eighty, but it wasn't. Her time on Earth was fifty-one years. I didn't have to like that fact—and I hate it, let me tell you—but I had to understand it.

Before that October, we weren't in denial, but we were moving forward with positivity and optimism. We knew the specific treatments we'd tried hadn't worked, but we felt hopeful we'd find a successful one. Then, that fall, the new circumstances hit us, and we had to come to terms and make peace with them. I had to recognize my kids would no longer have their mom, our friends and family would no longer have Margaret, and I'd no longer have my wife.

Margaret and I talked often as the days got closer to her death. She would say she was sad for me and the kids and felt sorry for the sadness left behind. I reassured her that we'd be fine, that the kids and I had each other. We'd cry together. During the last few months, I asked her how I could help her to smile again.

In her journal, she wrote, "John wants to know how to make me smile again. I just don't know. I get through the days, but when he gets home, he is the one I can talk to, and I feel bad because I'm such a downer. Lately, I feel I'm coming to my end. I'm weepy a lot. I want the pain gone. I want me back, and I don't know if that's real."

Before the end, Margaret herself also came to acceptance with her death. She felt ready. A strong woman of faith, she said she wasn't scared of dying, because she knew she'd have peace. For Margaret, the only thing she wasn't ready for was the sadness left behind—which, as you've learned from me and have now seen from my kids—is there, but we're going to be okay.

KELLY'S REFLECTIONS

Kelly was Margaret's college roommate and very close friend. She was wonderful because she'd always be in touch throughout Margaret's treatments. Whatever she could do to help, she did. Sometimes, she'd send little trinkets or flowers, or she'd stop by in person. Her support was consistent throughout the entire time Margaret was battling the disease. These are her reflections. They're important to share because they show another side of the journey.

I remember the day she [Margaret] called me and told me about what she later referred to as her cancer pain. She told me that morning when she woke up and tried to stand up and get ready for work, she doubled over in pain. I knew tests were going to happen. I knew it could be serious, but never in a million years thought it would be anything life-threatening.

I got the phone call about the diagnosis as I was getting out of my car to go to my daughter's tennis match. I remember standing in the parking lot, hearing Margaret's voice; it was a neuroendocrine tumor, slow growing, could've been there up to ten years. I remember her crying, saying she was scared.

I was looking off in the distance at all the people, and it was like everything was in slow motion. I could not believe what I was hearing. I was at a loss of what to say to comfort her, but somehow found the words that I prayed would help her not to be scared. I could hear the fear in her voice. I did not see Margaret cry for a very long time after that. She was scared, but she was tough.

I soon learned that I needed to follow Margaret's lead. She did not like to be peppered with questions about how she was feeling, her reaction to chemo, medicine, etc. I learned to ask more open-ended questions when we would text or talk on the phone: How is everything going? How is school? How are the kids doing? I knew that she wanted life to be as normal as possible for the kids. I knew she and John were carrying the weight of the world on their shoulders, but she did not want the kids to worry. Actually, she did not want anyone to worry about her. She was more concerned about making *other* people feel sad, so she often did not share how she was feeling or about the cancer.

＊ ＊ ＊

I can't remember the exact time period of all these next events, but for me, this is when the reality of how severe this was started to hit.

I distinctly recall my first visit to Boston with her to the hospital. We stayed with Marialice. I saw all the medication she had to take and the tracking she had to do. Sitting in the waiting room of the treatment center, everyone looked so normal to me, sitting there waiting to be called. I wondered how many of them were just like Margaret and wanted to be normal but found themselves with cancer, sitting in a waiting room waiting to see a doctor.

＊ ＊ ＊

Another time, I was heading to Albany for a conference, and she had to go to the hospital for intense
pain. Something told me I had to see her. I did not tell
her or John I was coming. As I approached the room,
I saw John sitting beside the bed. Margaret looked up
and smiled. She said, "Hi, bestie." I was so happy she
was happy to see me. I was happy that John was, too.
I always wanted to respect their privacy, but I needed
to see her. Once she got up to her room, John took a
well-needed break, and I stayed with Margaret. I was
happy to have the time alone with her. We walked up
and down the hallway. We talked about the kids. In
my heart, though, I looked at my best friend and kept
thinking, *Why is this happening to her?*

* * *

We took a trip to New York City just weeks before she
died. I remember looking over at her sleeping in the
car as we were driving to New York City and holding
back tears. Then, she woke up and told me she would
drive over the Tappan Zee Bridge and into Scarsdale
where her family lived. I was not sure she should be
driving—as she hadn't been doing that much—but she
was almost insistent. Something told me to just let her
do it. I pulled the car off to the side of the road before
the bridge. She got in the driver's side, we adjusted the
mirrors and the seat, and off we went. A couple times
she swerved a little, but I just held on. I knew I had to
let her drive. She drove all the way to [her sister] Gail's
office, right in the heart of Scarsdale. I remember telling
Gail when I got there that she drove, and she couldn't
believe it. I think Margaret knew it was her last time
driving over that bridge.

I went to mass with Margaret, her parents, and Gail
during that trip. Sitting in the pew together, it hit me:
I didn't want to leave. I didn't want to say goodbye. I
had to, though: John was coming down for the week-
end and taking her back home, and I had to head to

New Hampshire for my daughter's graduation. I hugged Margaret in the driveway. I told her I loved her. That was the last time I saw her.

* * *

Margaret called me the week before Christmas in the middle of the day. I was at work. I closed my office door, and she talked for about thirty minutes. She told me the conversation that she and John had to have with the kids. She cried. I cried. My friend was telling me she was going to die soon. Again, I didn't want to hang up. I didn't want the conversation to end, but it had to. That was the last time I heard her voice.

* * *

Butterflies and cardinals are my signs that Margaret's with me. A cardinal represents warmth, strength, and energy, and that we need to stay strong during difficult times. That was Margaret. I see cardinals all the time. I see yellow butterflies often when I'm out walking, and they always put a smile on my face. I feel like these are Margaret's messages to me.

Margaret would be so proud of John. He is such a great father and a great human being. I know that the kids are all getting older now, but keeping that connection to them helps me keep her alive. It comforts me to see how well the kids are doing and how John is working hard to move on with his life without Margaret. We all want him to be happy. I know Margaret does, too.

Thanks for this opportunity to reflect on my journey with Margaret throughout her illness. You're not going to believe this, but a butterfly just went through right up on my porch by me as I was typing this. She knows.

ROBIN'S REFLECTIONS

We met Robin after our daughters became friends way back in kindergarten, and we've been close as families ever since. In fact, I consider Robin and her husband, Dave, our best friends locally. Like Kelly, Robin did everything she could to help Margaret. These are her reflections.

There are so many ways I remember and honor Marg. Kelly—who, as you know, I've forged a bond with—and I enjoy each other's company and can talk about anything and everything...but especially about Margaret. We talk about our memories of her and how we still miss her tremendously today.

I keep a five-by-seven photo of Margaret and me together front and center on my dresser. The picture sits on top of the box you gave me with the wallet-sized picture of her in the corner of the frame, too. With the frame, I also keep a yellow rose from her funeral.

The last three years, whenever I went for a run, I did what I called my "mile for Margaret." The first mile I spent picturing her health, praying for her healing, and thinking of what a good friend she was. Today, I still dedicate a mile to Margaret, but I spend it differently: trying to hear [her] laugh, thinking about how much I miss her, visualizing her blooming with good health.

My observations of her illness are harder to put into words. Throughout the journey, it was so hard to face up to the fact that she was not going to live to [be] an old lady. The last year, I had to admit this to myself and change my thinking without upsetting Margaret. I was honored to be able to take her to Boston a couple times to help you out. I always tried to be there for her whenever she needed anything, especially with you at work and the kids at school. When we'd talk, I felt that she trusted me not to cry about things. She seemed to want to keep it private, just between you two and the kids, to a degree.

I don't know how you did it. Whenever I see a glorious sunset, I think of Marg. It's a Margie sky.

AN IMPORTANT NOTE

While I've shared in this chapter how Margaret and I talked to our kids about her illness at varying stages—and, at times, their reactions to and reflections on those conversations and tough moments—I know ours isn't the only way. There isn't a formula for this sort of thing.

In these cases, the most important thing is to know your kids. You have to understand the different personalities of your children and share information based on need and maturity level. Sometimes, you'll share more, and other times, you won't.

For example, we were able to share the most with Megan, our oldest. I still share with her often, to this day. It was hard on her, as you read, but she took the responsibility of helping her siblings to heart.

Harry has always been more middle-of-the-road. He was at an awkward age, those middle teen years, when we had many of our difficult conversations. I'd watch for signs to see if he struggled. I checked in with his lacrosse coach (see chapter four), too, who helped me by letting me know how he was doing.

Julia was the most sensitive out of all the kids. Because she was also the youngest, we didn't share as much with her outright. She lived the experience with us for six years until she graduated high school and went to college. Because she observed so much, less was said to her.

All in all, the kids knew they had Margaret and me, of course, but they also leaned on each other. I relied on Megan to help her brother and sister. Harry was helpful to Julia and would also reach out to Megan for support.

In short, communicating difficult news successfully requires knowing your kids and their different personalities. If you're facing this challenge, I suggest choosing what to share based on need and understanding. Your family dynamic will affect your approach; sometimes you need to disclose more than others. For us, as Margaret got closer to the end, we needed to share more. We needed to prepare the kids, so they weren't blindsided. They still felt strong emotions, but they had more information to understand what was happening. Such conversations are brutally tough but necessary.

Sometimes, you may only want to share enough to convey a basic understanding of what's happening. Other times, you may choose to be fully transparent. Each situation is different. We all have our own ways of dealing with tragedy, and my point in writing this book is not to offer a cookie-cutter approach. Oddly, grief is both a universal and individual feeling. Some people cave and feel victimized. Other people gain strength from protecting their children through the pain. I fall in the latter camp; my kids remain my first priority to this day, and I'm driven to keep them in a good place. It helps keep me going.

In short, when it comes to what difficult information to share and when to share it, it all comes down to knowing your kids and your family and assessing from there. You have to keep moving forward.

First recipient of the Margaret Sardella Lacrosse Scholarship, Dante Dewane, a former third-grade student of hers. (2017)

Margaret and her college roommate Kelly at Letchworth State Park. (July 2013)

Margaret and her sister Gail in NYC. (August 16, 2012, Margaret's birthday)

Margaret and John at the Grand Canyon for Margaret's fiftieth birthday.
(July 2015)

Margaret and John at the Corning Museum of Glass. (November 2016)

Margaret and John having a glass of wine. (July 2013)

Margaret and Julia on the beach at the Jersey shore. (February 2015)

Margaret and Marialice in Maine. (August 2013)

Margaret and Meg at Julia's lacrosse game. (October 2016)

Margaret and her good friend Robin at Robin's daughter's wedding. (July 2014)

Margaret meeting the Pope at a Catholic Women's Conference. It's really a cutout. Haha! (November 2015)

Margaret wearing yellow for her first IV chemo treatment. This was the day she received 100 pictures of support from friends and family wearing yellow. (December 2015)

Margaret, Harry, and Julia dropping Harry off to college for the first time.
(Keuka Lake 2013)

Our family dog Cortland, named for the college Margaret and I both attended and where we met. She loved that dog. (2015)

The Mrs. Sardella's Reading Corner in memory of Margaret at the school she taught at. It made sense to honor her this way because she loved her school, the students she taught, and reading. (Dedicated August 2018)

My buddies and I on our annual golf trip in January 2018 (Drac, La, Me, Gman, Swanny, brother Bill, and Mueller). These guys have always been there for me.

My buddy La (#40) and me (#10) on our 8th-grade basketball team (1977). Notice we are the same height? I'm standing on a bench, and he's on the floor. La was an important part of our journey, always as a friend first along with his guidance as a doctor.

Coach Felice and his wife Brit on their wedding day. Coach Felice is a great friend who was always there for support. (July 2015)

My girls, Margaret, Megan, and Julia in NYC on the Brooklyn Bridge. (2015)

Our three kids, Megan, Julia, and Harry. This is one of our favorite pictures of our kids. Harry is showing that he is three years old. (1998)

Our family Christmas. (2013)

Our family in Maine. (August 2013)

Our family at Julia's graduation party. (2016)

Sitting with John and Marialice Chipman at their lake house in Maine. We loved to visit and connect as families. It's one of our favorite places to go. (August 2015)

John coaching. The sport of lacrosse has always brought joy to our family. (2012)

One of my favorite school pictures of Margaret—one that is sitting in her reading corner to this day. (2014)

Chapter Four

CONNECTIONS: THE PLAYER, THE COACH, AND THE FRIEND

"Adversity does teach who your real friends are."

—LOIS MCMASTER BUJOLD

When you suffer a loss and move through grief, it can feel overwhelmingly heavy. So heavy, in fact, that sometimes you can't bear it all on your own. Human connection—*real* human connection—has always been sustaining to me, especially when I needed it most.

To illustrate the important connections in my life through losing Margaret, I'd like to tell you the stories of the player, the coach, and the friend.

THE PLAYER

I started coaching Bryan Capone in the third grade. I also mentored him as he grew up and matured into a great lacrosse player—specifically, our best defensive player. His senior year of high school, we won the sectional championship in double overtime—our first time in twenty-three years, beating the fifteen-time state champions we'd lost to the year before in triple overtime. We were hungry for it, and Bryan—leading the charge—knew it.

Bryan eventually landed a scholarship at the University of Vermont. Throughout those years as I guided him, Bryan would often ask me for letters of recommendation, which I was happy to give.

I supported him however I could, and that support did not stop when he went away to school. He had his ups and downs a little in college, as kids do, but I reminded him to keep his head up. We stayed in touch.

I remember his sophomore year, he was down because he was no longer starting. He'd been replaced. I saw his mother at the gym, and she gave me an update and asked if I'd give Bryan a pep talk. I did, of course. We had a special player-coach connection.

That same year, Bryan's coaching staff brought in a SEAL training program to help determine who the true leaders on the team really were. Personally, I knew Bryan was more than a solid player; he was the best leader I had ever coached. After the weeklong intensive training, the SEAL trainers evaluated all the players. Not surprisingly to me, Bryan was picked as the leader on his team. He became two-time team captain and did very well for himself. We continued to stay in contact.

After Margaret died, I was sitting in the family room when my phone rang. I had no idea who it would be. I hadn't talked to Bryan since the fall.

"Hey Coach, how are you?" I heard on the other end of the line. It was him.

"Coach, you've always been there for me," he continued. "Now, I'm here for you. Whatever you need."

I told him his words alone meant a lot, and that I'd let him know. Overall, the conversation itself was short and simple, but it was so powerful.

After I hung up, my kids—who had been sitting around me—asked who was on the other end of the line. I told them it was Bryan, and then I sat there and cried. I was overwhelmed by the support.

And there was more, too—Bryan and his brother were

there at the funeral, giving their physical presence, which is all too important. This story illustrates the power of our connection: he was always appreciative of everything I did for him, and I'm appreciative of what he did. It goes to show the power of the player-coach relationship—and how time tells a story.

THE COACH

I was the assistant lacrosse coach for many years under the head coach, Mike Felice. We have a lot more in common than that, though.

Mike is twenty years younger than I am, and his life parallels me and my kids' story. As a child, he grew up two doors down from my older brother, Billy. During that time, my brother had the opportunity to start a lacrosse program and coach many kids, including Mike, who was in elementary school and had just recovered from a battle with leukemia.

Mike underwent chemo for five years during elementary school. As he grew up, I remember him playing with my nieces, active and full of energy. He continued to play lacrosse and became a high school All-American before going on to play in college.

When Mike was a freshman in college, he was playing

in a game when a coach called him off the field and told him his mother had just died of cancer. He was eighteen years old. I remember talking with Mike—later, as adults—about his experience losing a parent while still a teenager. He shared he'd loved his mother deeply and felt all the emotions, including sadness, anger, loneliness, and confusion.

He continued to play lacrosse in college. In 2006 during his junior year, he scored the winning goal in the national championship game for Cortland State, which is also my alma mater. When he graduated from college, he started a teaching career in the same district I work in. We became friends and fellow coaches. Then, he took over the head coaching position, and I became one of his assistants.

At the same time, my wife was diagnosed with cancer. Mike was someone I turned to; he shared stories of his own experience with cancer as well as what it was like to live with his mother as she battled the disease. He understood what I was going through.

The year Mike took over as coach, we made it to the championship game for the first time in many years. Unfortunately, we lost in triple overtime. It was a heartbreaking loss, to say the least. The next year, we made it back to the championship game—and we won in overtime, bringing home the first championship in twenty-three years. All this goes to show Mike and I went through a lot together, on and off the field.

As we continued coaching together, my wife's cancer spread to her liver. At that point, it became inevitable that the disease would take her life. When she died, Coach Felice was there for me. He'd also been there for my son, coaching him through the years of Margaret's illness and also opening his heart to him after she passed. He recalls, "Seeing the change in Harry as a person and a player was something I kept an eye out for. I was able to have several deep, long conversations with him in regard to dealing with the emotion, the anger, and harnessing it into positive energy."

This came naturally to Mike, as he understood the difficulty of losing a mother at a young age. He could identify with my children, and he and I both feel like it's no accident we have been in each other's lives all these years. In particular, Mike has been a great influence on my son and helped him become the person he is today—someone with mental strength, the ability to move forward, a dedication to wellness and working out, and the grit to handle what comes his way.

Mike not only supported Harry, but also me and my wife. When Margaret was still alive, he talked to her about healthy foods to eat during treatment. They had a great connection, too, so he acted as a friend to the whole family. Margaret once asked him if he would take care of me after she was gone and ensure I stayed involved with coaching, which she knew was my form of therapy. As a principal, I worked all day putting out fires, but as a coach, I could teach again—teach kids the game and work on simple fundamentals, which felt empowering. Mike always gave me the room to play that role, with the utmost respect.

Margaret felt more at peace knowing I would continue coaching and Mike would be there for me. He understood the importance of support. He knew during my process, simple phone calls, texts, and face-to-face conversations could be very emotional. He was willing to listen to what I was going through. He stayed there for me, which built a special bond between us.

When I told Mike about this book and asked him to reflect on the support from his perspective, he talked about how it's not just the support itself that's important—it's the *consistency* of support. He said:

Once something like this happens, support comes out of the woodwork, and then gradually fades away to almost nobody. It's almost as if they feel as though they have done their job and that they do not need to check up on you anymore. That all of a sudden, time healed you and you are all good. I never wanted to be that person to you. I wanted to be the consistent support, checking in. Help that you need from the time the journey started, until we die together. Our sharing of lacrosse and coaching together made this very easy and very impactful.

We have so many connections and parallels, and he's in the relationship for the long haul, even though I'm now retired after thirty-four years of coaching. I hope by stepping aside, I can make room for a new young coach who can support him for the next twenty years. Of course, Mike and I still keep in touch. We're family. I went to his wedding, and he's going to my daughter's wedding. I see him being a dear friend for the rest of my life, which would make Margaret happy.

Life comes around in amazing ways. Mike was a child playing with my nieces when he was a young boy. He had cancer himself, and his mother died of cancer. My brother coached him, and then Mike coached with me. He supported me through the most difficult time of my life, when I lost my wife and the mother of my children. Today, Mike is still one of my most reliable friends and continues to be there for me every day.

THE FRIEND

When Margaret was diagnosed, seven friends were part of the journey right away. They supported us. I know these seven guys from elementary and middle school. I even went to kindergarten with two of them, and we were in the same class. We remain close to this day, and I'm fifty-six years old at the time of this writing. Our relationship spans more than fifty years.

When they found out about Margaret's diagnosis, they came over to my house. We had a barbecue. They acted like friends, helping keep life normal for me. The same is true after she passed. To this day, I know I can rely on them.

Included in this group is my buddy La, who I've mentioned before in this book. He's a doctor, but more importantly, he's a dear friend and served as a guide on our journey.

La and I became good friends when he was the center of our basketball team in eighth grade, and I was a guard. He was already 6'1" at that time, while I was 5'1". We often laugh about a picture I saved from that year. He's standing on the gym floor, and I'm standing on the bench. We're the same height.

Over the years, we've continued to grow closer as friends.

I was in his wedding party when he got married eighteen years ago. Around Christmastime, we would always go cut down our trees together. We took family trips to visit him when he lived in Chicago. His two boys are like little brothers to Harry. We've had a great relationship with his whole family, including his wife, Laura. Our friendship already had deep roots when my wife suddenly got diagnosed with cancer.

Around that time, my group of friends noticed I wasn't as communicative as normal. La called me. He asked me what was going on, and I opened up to him. He stepped right in.

In our situation, La had the freedom to use both aspects of himself—as a doctor and as a friend—without the need to keep himself at a professional distance (as he did with his regular patients). All the while, even when giving feedback, La remained supportive and respectful of all the doctors we worked with. He also told us Dr. Wong was one of the best and that we'd love him, which gave us confidence. When we went to Dana-Farber, he said it made perfect sense for us to join the clinical trial. He affirmed our choices and supported not only us, but his professional colleagues.

La also recognized the importance of networking. As a doctor, you don't make decisions alone; you make them by talking to other professionals about what you're seeing and trying. We found all the doctors consulted with each other to determine the best path moving forward. Mike's expertise is in working with patients with a variety of cancers, so he was familiar in this realm; he contributed to those treatment discussions without ever contradicting our providers or overstepping boundaries.

When I saw La last recently, I asked him how dealing with our situation helped him in his field. He said it made him a better doctor by understanding the patient experience side of the medical system. La says the conversations he has today with his patients are so much stronger than when he first started as a doctor. He understands the anxiety that cancer brings to each patient, he listens more, understands better, and is able to connect with each patient on a different level after watching Margaret and what she went through. It's just another way the power of human connection ties us all together.

QUALITY, NOT QUANTITY

Many people offered support after Margaret died. They constantly checked in to see how I was doing. After one month, I went back to work. The day-to-day routine helped my life maintain some normalcy; at the same time, people started to fade away. Every once in a while, I'd get a sympathy text from someone that said something like, "I know it's tough, but I hope you are okay."

Whenever I got expressions of sympathy like that, I thought to myself, Screw that. I don't need sympathy; I need support. I needed people to be physically present.

The people with me now are my family, closest childhood friends, fellow coaches, family friends, and a few others I've connected with. I don't need a lot of friends—I just need the right ones.

The three connections I've described in this chapter run deep and demonstrate the value I place on quality. I'm not interested in listing every single person I know, but rather in reflecting on the worth of the powerfully meaningful connections in my life. It's ironic, because I never would have experienced the strength of those relationships without going through this adversity. When you go through trials in life, you find out who your true friends are and the true connections you have. My philosophy is that the friendships and the connections I have may be fewer in number today than what I had five years ago—but they're more powerful now. My goal is to work every day to keep them stronger.

Chapter Five

MOVING FORWARD, HAVING HOPE

"Leaving family and friends is scary. I know I'll be in heaven. I believe that, but I don't want to leave yet. It hurts to think of John, Meg, Harry, and Julia without me. I know life goes on, it has to, I have lived that when friends and family have died. We mourn, but life continues. So back to my journey without a map, but allowing Jesus to lead me, comfort me, protect me."

—FROM MARGARET'S JOURNAL

When we lose someone, we can't stop living. You don't forget the person who passed away. Rather, you remember them every day as you continue to go through life. I learned this lesson from watching my mother.

As I was writing this book, my mom passed away at the

age of eighty-six, on April 28, 2019, more than sixteen years after my father died. When she died, I was by her bedside, along with other family members. When she passed, I knew she'd be in Heaven with my father. I smiled for her when she died, and my heart was full of happiness knowing she'd be reunited with him in a better place. To this day, I accept her passing. I was there for her, and I believe I was a good son to her.

It was difficult to watch her decline. She had two strokes and spent her last six months in a nursing home. She suffered from dementia and didn't recognize the people around her. She didn't eat or drink for about five months but kept hanging on. My siblings and I felt it was her time to go, and it was okay for her to die. We understood the situation and were ready for her to pass.

Losing Margaret helped me understand my mother more. I understand the hurt she endured during the last sixteen years of her life. She was married to my father for forty-eight years, and he was everything to her. She was an only child and didn't have any living family left on her side. She only had her four kids. She was sad, depressed, and lonely. My heart goes out to her and all others who have lost a partner they've connected with for so many years. I understand the feeling now.

My mother was the third person I watched die, but it was

the first time I actually smiled, because I knew she'd be with my father. I didn't shed a tear. I knew she was going to a good place, because my mother was a wonderful person with such high morals and values. It had been hard watching her retreat from the world and shut herself in over the years after losing her husband.

In short, my mother's passing brought me peace.

Having watched other people become paralyzed by grief, I told myself I couldn't do the same. I couldn't fall into the funk of drinking too much, staying home and not doing anything, or not facing my fear. After Margaret died, I knew how important it was for me to keep moving forward. As you know, I'd seen my own mother do the opposite after my father died. I knew I wouldn't do that to myself and my kids.

CLEANING THE BEDROOM

I didn't even try to clean out Margaret's classroom after she died, because I know I would've struggled too much. I didn't want to put the job on my kids, either, so a good friend cleaned that space for us and gave me the items. My house, though, was a different story.

The day Margaret died, I came home and looked around our bedroom. It was a place she spent time in often, especially as her strength weakened. There was so much sadness in the room. I filled two garbage bags full of medicine, tossing out at least twenty alone on her nightstand.

Cleaning her side of the bed and around her nightstand was when I broke down the worst. I felt like I couldn't breathe, so empty. What was ahead for me? I didn't know what was going to happen with the kids. How was I going to get through this? I'd lost the most important person in my life, a person who loved me unconditionally and who I had loved with all my heart.

After I cleaned the medicine, Julia and Megan went through Margaret's belongings along with Margaret's sister, Gail, in the room. Later, I emptied the room and filled it with new furniture.

I, of course, kept pictures of Margaret and other nostalgia on the walls. Some of the items hanging up in the bedroom stayed, like a watercolor we bought on our honeymoon in Bermuda's Horseshoe Bay. I tried to make sure the keepsakes I kept were visual ones with strong significance, but I made a point to reorganize them. I redid the space to move forward, but also to keep her memories alive. This choice served me well because it helped me to transform the room where she'd gone through most of her struggles with the illness. She was in bed all the time and took her medicines there. Changing the space gave me the power to figure out the balance of making sure I kept her memory alive within the house while still making it a space I could still live.

If you're living in the place where your loved one died, you might not even realize the paralysis of leaving the space the same as it was while they were still alive. You might feel guilty about cleaning out a closet or emptying a drawer, for example, but I found it was essential for me in this new chapter. It allowed me to start moving on in a respectful way. Trying to keep everything the same, on the other hand, can leave you in a kind of purgatory.

If you wonder why I cleaned the room so soon, it was out of necessity. It's a place I live in every day. Making those changes has helped me sleep at night.

THE QUOTE ON THE MIRROR

Our kids all stayed for that week of the funeral, but then my son, Harry, had to drive back to Myrtle Beach for college a week later. Ten days later, Julia had to go to college, too, for the second semester of her freshman year. After they left, Megan stayed with me for another week before driving back to New York City to continue her job. Once they'd all gone their respective ways, the loneliness crept in.

With the bedroom feeling like a different space, I decided to sit down and write a quote for myself—one I could look at every single morning to keep me motivated. I put it on the mirror in my bedroom. It read:

"Every day I wake up, I have a choice to make...Do I want to have a good day, or do I want to have a bad one? Do I want to be sad, mad, and have self-pity, or do I want to be happy? I have made the decision that I will have good days because that is the responsibility I have to my wife, to my kids, to my friends, and to all the people around me."

The quote worked so well for me because it gave me something to focus on. In those times, I would stay busy with the purpose to keep my mind off the pain and numbness of my experience. I took the quote down a year and a half later because I realized I didn't need to read it anymore—I was living it. I internalized the message on the mirror.

Today, the difference is that I stay busy not to take my mind off that experience, but just because that's what I do. Whatever I do every day, I make sure I have some kind of purpose. That purpose may be for others, or that purpose may be for myself.

When my kids are with me, for example, I pride myself

on making good dinners, eating together, and trying to keep some sense of normalcy. I used to be the barbecue guy; I'd barbecue the food, and Margaret would make the rest of the dinner. Now, I make the complete dinner. I think of her when I make it. I say to myself, *Okay, I've got to make sure I have the greens for balance.* Those little activities make a difference for me.

Ultimately, I know that moving forward is a tribute to those we've lost. You don't forget the person who passed away, but you remember them every day as you continue to go through life.

LITTLE REMINDERS

After Margaret passed, I received hundreds of sympathy cards, prayer cards, mass cards—you name it. As a principal, I was a visible community member, and she was a teacher in the district. I read every one of them and then put them away. As more notes and reminders came in over the following couple of years, I'd read and store them away, too. The first time I revisited everything was to write this book, which is how I found the note from Beth I shared in the first chapter.

In general, I don't go in it and reread these keepsakes. It's not like rereading old love notes or looking at other reminders from a good time of my life. Still, I kept the items people sent me. The container with all the notes is down in the basement.

When people think they're being sentimental and sending me a card these days, I put those in the container, too. It's very difficult to open those cards upon the anniversary of her death or her birthday.

I know people want to support me and my family, which is kind. I know people send notes to express their sympathy. Many times, I've sent sympathy cards and reached out to other people myself. Still, I had to compartmentalize that piece of my experience by putting the cards away. The container is full, and I appreciate the gesture, just as I did the outpouring of support at the wake and funeral.

I still get other in-person reminders, too. People I haven't seen in a while say, "I'm so sorry to hear about your wife." Those reminders come often, and they are always sincere. However, I'm trying *not* to be reminded, because I already have the thought in my head. It's already there. It doesn't stop.

The other side of reminders seems to be silence. Margaret's family doesn't talk about her death much. My brothers and sisters don't really talk about it, either. Certain friends, like the ones I discussed in chapter four, can talk about it because they understand what I'm going through—largely through their own life experiences.

What I want is what's between the sympathy and the silence—*life*. Normalcy. Authenticity. I'm writing this book to share our journey and help people who are facing a loss or supporting someone facing a loss. Communication is a big part of that. When people tell me today that they just don't know what to say to me, I reply, "Just be normal and talk to me like you've always talked to me." If Margaret comes up, she comes up—it's okay. Being married to her and then losing her are parts of my life, and it's okay to talk about her.

MARGARET'S JOURNAL

The toughest part of moving forward was reading Margaret's journal. I knew she was keeping it throughout her journey. When she died, I put it in a bottom drawer and let it sit there, knowing someday I'd have to look at it. Margaret chronicled everything, from her diagnosis to her final days. I've shared some passages within this book, which shine a light on who she was: a loving mother, devoted daughter, sister, and friend who had a strong spiritual strength.

When I first tried to read her journal about a year after she passed, the experience was so emotional I don't even know how to put words to it. I could only get through a couple of pages. I put it away and drove over to our friend Robin's house and sat down with her and her husband, Dave, to talk. It was the first time I opened up to them after my wife's death. They knew I didn't share a lot naturally, but that night, we talked about Margaret and her journal, had some wine, and cried. They were there for me.

As emotional as it was, reading it also helped me move forward. When I started thinking about this book, I thought maybe the journal would form a story thread within it or the basis for one of the chapters; that idea became what you're reading now. The process has been cathartic for me. Even though the chronicle has taken me through some serious emotional ups and downs, it has also deepened her memory and our connection.

If you feel paralyzed by loss, I recommend surrounding yourself with good people. If you're a person who wants to share your experience, either do it in written form or verbally with people you trust. It's helped me out tremendously to write this story down. I'm in such a better place because of the process—it's incredible. I'd already grappled with the experience and my thoughts about it in my head for years, as well as through therapy. But the process of writing it down, organizing my thoughts, and making sense of the big picture is transformative. I've had the chance to share Margaret as a person and have deeper, more powerful, and more complete conversations that put all the pieces together.

STRENGTH, NOT REPRESSION

The first eight months after losing Margaret, I felt numb. I went through the motions and stayed busy, just to keep my mind going. At eight months, I started falling into a depression. I visited friends at their house out on the ocean by Boston, and I felt lonely and down.

When I came home, I knew I needed the help of a therapist. I asked a few professionals for their advice and received the name of an expert in grief. She was wonderful and helped me through this difficult time. We met weekly until we could meet less frequently. Now, I only reach out to her as needed, which has only happened a couple of times this year.

I am better today, but I still experience intensified grief during special milestones, such as our anniversary, Margaret's birthday, holidays, and get-togethers. The anniversary of her death is the most difficult time, because it represents one more year of her not being here, which gives a sense of distance.

When a special celebration happens, such as a wedding,

I feel empty. I look out at the married couple and realize that I don't have that connection anymore. The knowledge overwhelms me and creates loneliness. I retreat and get away from the group. I'm ready to go, because the event evokes sadness for me. My friend Robin once told me, "It's a couple's world," and she's right.

Some questions that still come to the forefront for me are: Why did this happen to my wife? Why has this happened to me? What am I going to do today to keep busy and keep my mind going? How can I be a good father to my kids? Am I making the right decisions for myself and for them? My kids will always come first. I always try to be as mentally strong as I can, without giving in or playing a victim.

By strength, I don't mean repression. That's an important designation. It's important to have room to acknowledge your grief. It's not normal to avoid the full array of emotions. I have a saying: "You can have a pity party, but don't let the pity party last too long." If you're not careful, you can get into a funk. For me, there are still days when I struggle, especially during milestones. The key for me is that the next day, I know I need to wake up continuing to move forward.

I'm committed to developing as a person and always being stronger emotionally as I grow. Some people think being emotionally strong means not showing your emotions;

I disagree. Feel them, show them if you're comfortable, and keep going.

MY LIFE TODAY

Upon death, the world keeps moving around you. I watched my wife live a shortened life, and I decided life itself is too short. I want to end my years on my own terms.

Upon my retirement after thirty-one years in education, I traveled and bought a condo in Naples, Florida. I see my kids, siblings, and friends often. I focus on strengthening the important relationships in my life. As you know by now, I don't need a lot of friends; I just need the right ones.

I've found that as I've moved through my grief, what I've needed from people has evolved over time. Even as I described the people who weren't able to provide the kind of support I needed in the moment, there are absolutely no hard feelings. It's not their fault, nor is it my fault. Some people are unable to be physically present or simply don't know what to say. I definitely live in a lonelier time now, but I understand it.

For example, Margaret and I used to do a dinner club together with four other couples. The wives always made the connections. As for my part, I'd go along for the ride and drink all the wine. With Margaret gone, now it doesn't work that way. I don't get those invitations, because the connection is simply not there anymore.

Do I even want those dinner invitations? I'm not sure. I fight with a contradiction: it would be nice to still be included, but I also know the experience would feel empty for me, because I'm missing something important—my partner. I don't like being the third wheel.

When it comes to my close connections, though, I'm okay attending on my own. If Dave and Robin ever invited me out, for example, I'd say yes in a heartbeat. I feel so comfortable with them, because they're two of the closest friends I have as a couple. To me, spending time with them is perfectly normal. They bought a place right after I did down in Naples, Florida, and we do activities together as a group of three, such as going to the beach or playing golf. They're like family.

When you make a connection with the right person (or people), it's amazing how many similarities you have and the power of the relationship to last a lifetime. I have leaned on those connections in the past, and I still do today. That's what keeps me going—finding purpose every day, living my life on my own terms, and making Margaret proud.

KEEPING MEMORY ALIVE

With close friends, I share how I miss my wife. I miss her gentle touch, her gentle way, her unconditional love. I miss that she can't be there for our kids' weddings and other special events and milestones. Harry graduated after she died, so she couldn't celebrate that accomplishment with him. She missed Julia's lacrosse seasons and college experience. She missed Megan's engagement and upcoming wedding. Thinking about her absence from those important events makes me feel empty. There's no other way to describe it.

For me, I try to use grief as fuel by channeling my great memories of the person I've lost into a legacy that can help others. I have the idea of creating the Yellow Sneaker Fund, which would be a foundation to raise money for other people who have gone through our experience of loss. When Margaret passed away, I told the kids we would spend the next Christmas—as December has always been a hard month for our family—on vacation. We ended up going on a cruise. The four of us were together, and we got our minds off of the holiday situation and the loss of Margaret not being there by having a new destination to explore. We ended up having a wonderful vacation together.

I imagine the Yellow Sneaker Fundraising money to give other people who have gone through a similar situation an opportunity to get away for a few days. I'd like to help people have happiness, even if it's for a short period of time.

I've also memorialized Margaret through the Margaret Sardella Lacrosse Scholarship. Lacrosse has always been special to our family. I've been part of the game as a player, a coach, an administrator, and more for almost fifty years. I've written books on the game, and it's been very important in my life. My kids have all played since they were young, and my daughters have played the sport in college. When our youngest daughter was in high school, Margaret was the booster club president and helped wherever she could with the program. She was a big fan of the sport and watched hundreds of games played by our children and coached by me.

When she passed, I created a lacrosse scholarship in her name for both the boys' and girls' lacrosse programs, giving $500 to each recipient. Each year, a graduating senior gets this assistance to help with their transition to college. Of the eleven that have been awarded at the time of this writing, three recipients have been Margaret's former students—something that's especially meaningful to me.

Another way Margaret has been memorialized is through the creation of Mrs. Sardella's Reading Corner in the library at the school where she served as a third-grade teacher for more than ten years. It's a beautiful space, decked out in yellow. In my heart, I know she loves it.

A BALANCED LIFE: FAITH, FAMILY, AND FRIENDS

Margaret and I attended the same church, Pope John XXIII, for our whole twenty-seven years together, although I didn't convert to Catholicism until later in our marriage. When Margaret was first diagnosed with cancer, she felt compelled to share the news with Father O'Brien, our priest, which began a special relationship for her and our family. I remember him saying to me the journey ahead would be a challenging one—and man, was he right. As Margaret recalled in her journal, "Father O'Brien said, 'You did all the right things with your disease, you look to your faith, and you are supported by family and friends.' He's seen them come to church with me."

As time went by, the importance of attending church and strengthening our faith was important to all of us. Even before her diagnosis, Margaret was exceptionally active in the church; she attended daily mass Monday through Friday, was a faith formation teacher, was a Eucharistic minister, and even served on our parish council. Margaret's faith had such a powerful religious impact on me that I decided in 2006 to participate in the Rite of Christian Initiation of Adults (RCIA) program, because I was a Protestant and converted to Catholicism. I also participated with my youngest daughter when she was taking her first communion at the Easter vigil that year. It turned out to be a very special memory for us.

I believe faith is a core component to a balanced life. Through Margaret and her family, I learned the importance of having a strong faith and a relationship with God. Mine happens to be through my Catholic faith. When I talk about faith, though, please understand that I am talking about spiritual connection. Everybody has a different one. Some people pray to the Buddha or have a more reflective practice connected to the Earth, like Taoism. The spiritual piece means knowing there's more out there. It gives you something to believe in. Whether you go to church, meditate, practice yoga, or find other avenues of spirituality, I believe faith is a large part of what balances us.

I've always tried to work on having a balanced life. I see the importance of strengthening every component of that balance, which includes my faith, family, friends, and integrity. Preparing for a balanced life prepared me to handle the most difficult situations, including Margaret's. At the end of the day, the moments that shape you are not materialistic—they're real. They have a profound effect on you because they're part of the deeper human experience. As a leader, I've found that people who struggle and can't handle the hardest challenges are truly imbalanced in their life. They're missing at least one component of balance.

In addition to faith, family, friends, and integrity, I also think it's important to pursue a passion. I pursued a passion for the game of lacrosse by coaching it. It gave me that outlet. I also find passion in music and writing, which allows me to try to define who I am through reflection.

The truth is that it's hard to keep all the cylinders of a balanced life firing all the time. You have to work at it every day. It's like hitting the gym and lifting weights; you have to lift more weight to get more muscle. The work means looking yourself in the mirror and asking, "What are the things I'm doing, and are they the right ones to do?" You reflect and move forward. Some days, maybe you have to work a little harder than others. Some days, balance just comes naturally. The reality is, you have to keep reminding yourself of the components of a full life—especially when you've suffered a loss.

Margaret already had many of the qualities of a balanced life. Still, through her illness, she became stronger in her faith. She was already the best wife, mother, and friend people could ever want. I knew I had somebody special. I just didn't realize the full effect she had on my life until she died.

As I write this today, I'm okay with dying because I know I'll be with her again. I don't want to leave too soon, because I know my kids would struggle with grief and loneliness. At the same time, I look forward to partnering with her again one day. The promise of Heaven brings comfort and peace to me. When I'm in a plane, I feel closer to her. This is because of my faith.

REGAINING BALANCE

When Margaret died, I lost balance because I lost her as a person. To this day, on some level, I'm still trying to find my equilibrium.

To help regain my balance, I've been connecting with people locally who are going through their own challenging situations. For example, I've been in constant contact with a friend whose husband has been close to death; sadly, he passed away while I was writing this book. I have been checking in with her, seeing how she's doing, and helping guide her through parts of the process. I've also reached out to others who are going through a difficult time with cancer. Reaching out to others, particularly through this book, gives me purpose.

Recently, I went out with my son and his friends to watch the Syracuse football game, and his friend's dad joined us. A year ago, this man's wife died of breast cancer at age fifty-eight. The father—a quiet, reserved man—sat with me. We don't connect a lot, but were having a normal conversation. When I asked him how he was *really* doing, he opened up. I remember him looking at me as we were having an emotional conversation and saying, "I know you understand."

He said he's lost his balance and feels confused. He said he's afraid of bringing other people down.

I did, indeed, understand all of that. Very well.

We talked through all those concerns. The father also mentioned he was thinking about the first anniversary of his wife's passing—a milestone that was quickly approaching. I could tell he felt anxiety and angst around that milestone. I explained that for me, the day itself isn't always the toughest day; it's the buildup to it. I'm coming up on the third anniversary of Margaret's death, and I still feel the dread—I just know how to manage it better. And now, I'm in a place to help others do the same. It's how I move forward.

Chapter Six

WALKING ON BINNEY STREET: THE LEGACY YOU LEAVE BEHIND

"John took off all of December to be with me. What more can I say. We're like an old retired couple. I just don't want to leave him alone."

"'Walking on Binney Street'—that's the title of the book John wants to write with me. He continues to be supportive and makes me laugh. Thank goodness for him."

—FROM MARGARET'S JOURNAL

When Margaret was diagnosed with cancer, the doctors decided her first step was to go to Dana-Farber Cancer Institute in Boston. At the time, we didn't realize how much importance this institution would hold in our journey together. Every other Thursday, we drove to Boston, stayed with our good friends the Chipmans, and drove to Dana-Farber for her appointment the next day. Sometimes we were there for an hour, other times for the whole day.

While waiting to see the doctor before or after an appointment, we took many walks up and down the streets of Boston, and it seemed we always ended up on one in particular: Binney Street. We would joke that one day, our story would be titled *Walking on Binney Street*.

BINNEY STREET

Binney Street holds meaning for me because it felt simple but meaningful that we always ended up on it—and not always on purpose. As one of the four streets surrounding Dana-Farber, it seemed like whenever we looked up at a street sign, we found ourselves there. We'd wander in close proximity to the hospital, and suddenly we'd realize, "There's Binney Street again."

In her journal, Margaret joked about how during one visit when she had to drink medicine for the CAT scan, she had to stay near a bathroom because the medicine would go through her quickly. I remember that particular visit, when we saw Binney Street again, she said, "Here we go, pooping on Binney Street."

God, she was funny. We'd laugh together often. That place—that hospital, and that street in particular—holds a lot of special memories.

THE THREE PEOPLE I'LL NEVER FORGET

During Margaret's treatment, our world revolved around leaving work for a day and traveling to Boston. Along with my wife's appointments during these times, we also got a big dose of perspective.

While we went through this monumental challenge, others still attended to their daily routines. They didn't have a clue what we were experiencing, which was okay—I hope they never go through the same trials. On the other hand, we also learned some people had it even worse than we did.

There are three people I'll never forget from that time.

The Child in a Wheelchair

After Margaret and I parked the car at Dana-Farber for one of her biweekly visits, we walked over to the elevator to go up to her appointment. As we approached, we saw a young mother with three children. One of them was around ten years old and in a wheelchair. He was frail and had a mask on, and his eyes looked sad. I waved to him, and he gave me a wave back.

The mother seemed very anxious and unsure of what to do, so Margaret and I helped give her directions. I told her it would be okay and showed her what we knew about how the building worked. She appreciated our help and went on her way, pushing the child in the wheelchair.

I wonder where that child is today. Did he survive? Did he pass away? I don't know, but I know that day we made a small difference for him, his mother, and his two younger siblings. And he made a difference for us.

The Man with Half a Face

Once, as we waited for Margaret's blood work, I watched the many people around us. I noticed one man who was also waiting. He had yellowish skin—and, as I looked closer, I realized he was missing half his jawbone.

Seeing this man gave me immediate perspective that we weren't the only ones going through this journey, and it showed me others have it worse.

The Angry Woman

Once, as we were waiting for Margaret to have her bimonthly CT scan, an older gentleman—one of many volunteers at Dana-Farber—was walking around asking people if they wanted a copy of the newspaper. He said the same thing over and over, in a positive, kidding voice: "Hi! Do you want some good news, or some bad news?"

I watched as a woman, clearly angry, turned to him and said, "I don't need any bad news. I already have heard enough bad news."

The volunteer, who was then unsure of what to say, hung his head and walked away.

I vividly recall that as I watched this scene unfold in front of me, I felt for both of them. One person was trying to help, and the other was angry at the world because she was facing a tragic disease. But really, they were both trying their best in that moment.

THE BEAMS

When I was younger, I'd often see ads for Dana-Farber at the movie theater, raising money for the Jimmy Fund—a program supporting pediatric cancer research. Afterward, the ushers would walk around with a canister to collect spare change.

That was the extent of what I knew about Dana-Farber back then—those memories of the movie theater, the commercials. I always wondered what Dana-Farber was all about. Then, when Margaret was diagnosed, I got my answer.

Dana-Farber is one of the most powerful places I've ever experienced. The building provides hope for others. At times, there would be hundreds of people waiting for blood work, something Margaret had to do every time she was there. We'd then go meet with the doctor, who was a wonderful person with a calming and caring demeanor. I will always give her credit for the work she does.

Margaret's first clinical trial was successful in stabilizing the cancer so that it didn't progress. All her appointments at that time were at the old building, as the new one was being built right across the street.

When we visited the *new* Dana-Farber building, it had quite a different feel. As you walked in the entrance, you could see a piano that stood in the main vestibule so people could play and hear beautiful, soothing music. It also had a number of symbolic displays, many of which were donated by patients' families: the gene display explaining the genetic component of cancer, the artwork, the Stoneman Healing Garden.

There were also names spray-painted on the exposed beams. Those hit me the hardest.

I remember walking down a stairwell, looking up at the beams, and thinking *Who would spray paint beams with graffiti in such a special place?* Then, I opened the doors, and I understood. I learned the story: when the steel-workers were constructing the new Dana-Farber building, they'd see patients standing in the windows of the old building. These patients, including children, would hold up their names against the windows, and the steelworkers would spray paint them on the beams. What Margaret and I were seeing were names of cancer patients through-out the building, whether they lived or died. Real people with real stories.

Seeing those beams got to me. I realized that the brick and mortar of the building didn't make the place special; the people in it and those who share their spirit do. The true meaning of that building lies in providing hope to people who are struggling. The institute truly does make a difference for others. Over the years, I've thought about our visits to Dana-Farber. I hold that facility as one of the most memorable I've ever visited—a place of caring, hope, and making a difference for many.

When you consider your life—what you've done and what you intend to do with the time God gives you—it's import-ant to consider the legacy you leave behind. I believe a legacy is based on how you live. Did you do the right thing? Did you help others when they needed it the most? Did you make a difference in someone's life?

As I wrote about the names on the beams at Dana-Farber,

I believe my name is on the beams where I made a difference: my family, my friends, the school district where I worked, my community, and on the lives of those I coached in the game of lacrosse.

I hope this book also helps others through a difficult time. As you read this, think about which beams your name will be on. Where have you made a difference?

I know what my legacy is. Do you know yours?

CONCLUSION

I always knew I wanted to write a book, but I thought it would just be a book of impactful stories of my experiences in life. I thought I'd include family, friends, life and work experiences, coaching stories, and so on. When I finally began sharing those stories and ideas, though, I realized the real thread was about Margaret and me working through her illness together.

I hope you, as a reader, can benefit from some of the lessons I learned and encouragement I gave myself over the last ten years. My experience shows as difficult as it may feel, you can keep living. Often, I've told myself, "Life doesn't stop. You've got to keep moving forward." When you face adversity, it's important to find ways to help others and keep progressing.

In my job as a principal and as a coach, I've learned I can be a mentor to others and the way I act can influence others. I've always felt drawn toward creating something to share. What you're reading now is another example of that.

When I tell people parts of my story, they often had no idea what I've been through. They'll say, "Wow, you're doing so well!"

And I am! But I also have days that are hard. I've found that sharing, in itself, can be cathartic. When you share your story, you open up the opportunity to connect with other people and have a deeper dialogue. Even if people haven't experienced exactly what you have, they can take a piece of your story and connect with it.

Over the years, I've learned that many of the challenges we go through in life can feel like a bucket of water in the ocean—but when I lost Margaret, she *was* my ocean. Some days without my wife are harder than others, but they're all opportunities to keep going.

Losing Margaret taught me a lot, including showing me the important people in my life who could stay present with me when things got tough. It reinforced the power of human connection. It taught me we can get through this, together.

In that spirit of connection, you have an open invitation to email me at Ajourneywithoutamap@gmail.com, find me on Twitter at @sardella_john, or visit johnsardella.com

I hope you see now that you're on a journey. You might not yet know which direction you're going in. And that's okay. You're going to be okay. We all are. It's just another journey without a map.

ACKNOWLEDGMENTS

I would like to thank the following people for their contributions to this book. Thank you for your support over the years. You all make a difference.

- My kids: Megan, Harry, and Julia
- Gail Leone
- Marialice and John Chipman
- Ben Chipman
- Beth Lozier
- Mike Felice
- Bryan Capone
- Mike LaCombe
- Robin and Dave Chalifoux
- Kelly Sattora
- Maureen Woods
- Father O'Brien

- Dr. Chan and the staff at Dana Farber
- Dr. Wong and the staff at Hematology-Oncology Association of CNY
- The staffs of Willow Field Elementary School, Soule Road Elementary School, and the Liverpool CSD

ABOUT THE AUTHOR

JOHN SARDELLA is the author of two previous books: *How to Start a Successful Youth Lacrosse Program* and *L is for Lacrosse: An ABC Book*. John's professional career was spent in the Liverpool CSD. He was a teacher for sixteen years and a principal for fifteen years. He is now retired and enjoys spending his time writing, golfing, and being with family and friends. John resides in Liverpool, New York, and Naples, Florida. His kids are all grown, and John still sees them often. You can find John on Twitter @sardella_john, connect via email at ajourneywithoutamap@gmail.com, or visit johnsardella.com.

CPSIA information can be obtained
at www.ICGtesting.com
Printed in the USA
JSHW021226300120
3910JS00001B/9